The Real Goal

An Operational Excellence Novel

Terry L. Campbell

James Camerer, Jr.

James M. Guyette, Jr.

DEDICATION

To all of you who have worked for Duke.

ACKNOWLEDGMENTS

We would like to thank our clients.
Without you there would be no us.

Thank you for your trust.

Foreword by Lt. General (Ret.) William (Gus) Pagonis

The best leaders have the combined traits of expertise and empathy. Once leaders are identified they must continually improve - if one expects to be successful in both the military and civilian worlds. The authors have taken a unique approach to illustrating operational excellence. By reviewing systems, promoting leadership, collaboratively solving problems and then sharing knowledge organizations can better serve customers – The Real Goal of business. The techniques are illustrated in real world examples. An easy read that proves to be interesting and informative.

Foreword by the Authors

The combined characteristics of expertise and empathy are rare in leaders. When you find a leader who possesses both traits, listen, learn and grow. These are individuals who understand the fundamental balance of being a learner, being a leader and being alive. This is the story of a new leader who discovers the Real Goal.

Nothing creates problems like solutions.

1

"You're quitting?"

"Effective immediately," replied Gary.

Dwight "Duke" Regus couldn't believe what he was hearing. This was the last piece of bad news he needed to complete a week full of disappointments.

"Gary, I know I've been riding you hard about the operational issues in your area. Can you at least give me two weeks to find your replacement?" pleaded Duke.

"Look Mr. Regus, you told me if the problems in picking and packing didn't disappear than I would be disappearing. Well, I took that motivational speech as an incentive to find a new job. Next week I am going hunting which is a vacation I planned months ago so in effect I am giving you a week's notice. I start at Maltese Logistics in two weeks."

"You're going to the competition?"

Duke's thinning jet black hair was slicked straight back. The lines on his forehead yielded to what looked like one lonely long bushy salt and pepper eyebrow that was really two overgrown eyebrows in need of pruning. His bulging middle showed just how much he enjoyed pasta and deserts. The two lower buttons on his shirt fought to keep hidden his bare stomach. His face reddened as the blood raced to his head.

Gary tried to be professional. He presented a very flattering resignation letter, complimenting his boss, his peers and all the folks he worked with over the past 3 years. But as with many interactions with Duke they digressed to children fighting over a ball on the playground. When Duke did not get his way through negotiation he got it through intimidation.

Today Gary would not be intimidated. It wasn't his nature to fight back but he had had enough of Duke's management style.

"I am going where my contributions will be recognized and rewarded and to where I will have a career.

I'm going to where…" Before Gary could finish Duke was on the speakerphone.

"Linda, send security to my office to escort Mr. Madowski out of the building."

"Yes, Mr. Regus, right away." Linda responded with authority.

Gary lost his train of thought. Three years of dedication and loyalty were going to end with security unceremoniously dumping him out of the building? Subconsciously he knew it wouldn't end well and at the best it would be awkward. When he accepted the offer a month ago he slowly began taking his personal items home. The last and only thing left were the items in his pockets and the picture of his family on his screen saver.

Security arrived before any more words were spoken. Before Duke looked up again his office was empty.

Softly, but with authority and composure, Duke, said, "Linda, please have my management team assembled in my conference room for an urgent meeting." Duke had three types of meetings: staff, emergency and urgent, in reverse order of priority.

Linda had worked for Duke since the company had expanded to Chicago. She knew to listen to the subtle queues in language that determined the difference between the possessive "my management team" and "the management team". 'The management' team meant all twelve of his managers. 'My management' team meant his inner circle: Don the Financial Controller, Mike his loyal assistant GM, Patrick his operations manager, sometimes, John, his son in law, but never his HR manager Sheila. John was invited to emergency meetings but not urgent meetings. Sheila was only invited to staff meetings.

Professional courtesy dictated that Linda ask what the meeting topic was so she could relay the subject to his inner circle but she already knew. And by now the whole company probably knew.

"Mr. Regus, can I give them a meeting subject so they can come prepared?"

"Were going to make some succession planning decisions."

"Very good sir."

Duke couldn't believe how terrible his week had been. The owners were all over him because he was over budget in overtime, way over budget. His customers were on him about his operational issues that were affecting their customers. And to top it off his wife was angry because the marble tile they were installing in the kitchen did not have the same hue of pink they had seen in the showroom.

Mostly accused of being a pessimist Duke was a realist. He knew that once he turned this place around he would be rewarded with a return to corporate in Florida or better yet, heading up the new facility rumored to be in Savannah. Either would be better than the winters here in Chicago.

The realist in him told him he needed to prepare for his urgent meeting. He could not tell his inner circle everything that was going on. That would breed chaos. But they needed to get the message that this situation with their customer was critical.

On Monday MDG told him they were considering invoking the early termination clause in their third party logistics contract. Not even knowing what the terms of that clause were Duke knew it was not good. He assured MDG that operational issues were start-up related and would be resolved immediately and that invoking the clause would not be necessary. After the call he pulled up the contract to find out what the termination clause said.

Amongst all the legalese was something that said MDG had the right to terminate the contract with three months notice if independent auditors proved they were not working to the terms of the agreement.

His inner circle had already been left waiting too long. Duke went into the meeting without a formal agenda or specific plan about how to relay the information. Two topics had to be covered: The impending visit of MDG and the replacement for Gary.

The discussions ceased as soon as the conference room door opened. Without any salutations Duke took his seat at the head of the conference room table. Without eye contact he said, "We have two urgent issues to discuss: 1. MDG visit next week and 2. Gary's replacement. These issues are related because Gary has always been our point person when hosting MDG for their site visits. They respect his knowledge of the process and they like him. But first things first. What are we going to tell MDG about our corrective action plan to solve the operational issues that have been plaguing us since the start-up?"

"We have just implemented a final inspection station. I suspect all issues will disappear immediately," responded Patrick.

"Don what's that going to do to our headcount budget?" asked Mike.

"Obviously that's going to put us over budget. We never forecasted for a final inspection line." Replied Don.

Duke didn't care about budgets. His bonus was determined by EBITDA. This final inspection station would not be a part of the adjusted EBITDA calculation when it came time to discuss his bonus.

Mike's bonus was determined by meeting budgets. Duke was confident he would find a way to shuffle around the different buckets of money to accommodate this headcount change and still meet budget.

"This meeting is not about budgets. It's about ensuring we have a corrective action plan that will satisfy our customer when they arrive next week," Duke interjected with authority to bring them back to the subject.

"Patrick if you're confident in your new inspection process the next topic is what do we tell the client about Gary?"

Mike responded, "Why don't we tell them the truth? Gary is on vacation next week."

"Oh good idea, yeah, he's been planning that hunting trip for awhile. The customer won't ever suspect a thing." Said Patrick.

"Great idea. Now then last decision, who do we promote to replace Gary?" Duke asked.

"Frankie."

"Yeah, good idea."

"Who's Frankie?" asked Duke.

"Frankie? Great choice. Knowledgeable, respected. Very thorough and detail-oriented. Will climb the learning curve quickly."

Duke had no idea who Frankie was or that this meeting would be so easy. Corrective action plan for client, check. Replacement for Gary, check. Maybe he would make that afternoon tee time after all.

"Patrick, send Frankie to my office immediately. Meeting adjourned."

2

Fall seemed to come earlier and earlier the longer Duke lived in Chicago. It wasn't like Florida where he could golf year round. He was determined to get a few more rounds in before Mother Nature turned on him.

Duke was not much of a golfer but he enjoyed the camaraderie of sharing war stories with other executives like himself. This was his first year as a full member of the Clayton Springs Country Club. He was going to get his money's worth by playing as many rounds as possible.

He wondered who would be a part of his foursome today. Would it be that divorce lawyer that was full of good gossip? Or maybe that Operations VP from the car company? Duke would love to land their account. As he strategized how to attack the fourth hole water hazard he heard a firm knock on his door.

"Come on in," bellowed Duke.

As soon as Duke realized it was no one he was expecting he said, "Thanks for coming in. You know I have an open door policy but I'm expecting someone and have an important meeting. Please make an appointment with Linda."

"Forgive me for barging in but your assistant is not here and I was told to come to your office."

"You were? By whom?"

"Patrick. Well not directly. He told my supervisor and my supervisor told me. I'm Frankie."

"You're Frankie?" asked Duke incredulously.

"Yes. Francis Cabrini but everyone calls me Frankie."

Trying to feign his surprise he said "Nice to meet you, Frankie."

"Oh we met before. You came out to the picking area the last time the customer was here and you introduced yourself."

"Yes, of course, I remember." Of course he didn't remember. All he could remember from that visit was kissing his customer's ass for three straight hours. Telling them how productivity is improving but not mentioning that quality is digressing.

The chiming of his cell phone was the lifeline he needed. "Frankie could you give me a moment. I have to take this call and then we can continue our discussion. Why don't you wait in the conference room? Help yourself to coffee and refreshments and I will join you after this call."

It was his wife calling. He had no intention of answering it to find out what the home crisis du jour was. He hit decline call. Then quickly speed dialed Mike.

Mike answered on the first ring. He liked that about Mike. It didn't matter if it was morning, noon or night. Mike was ready to execute his orders.

"Hello, Duke."

"Mike I don't remember you telling me Frankie was a woman. And you certainly didn't tell me she was black!"

"I…well, Duke, I didn't think it was important," Stammered Mike.

"Well in the politically correct sense it doesn't matter. But…but will she be respected? Will the guys follow her orders?"

"Oh! Of course. I mean…you heard everyone was in agreement that she was the best person to succeed Gary. She's very knowledgeable of the picking process and she's a grade 8 picker and packer. If the union didn't make us promote on seniority she would have been a grade 10 months ago and…"

14

"Mike I guess the point is I don't like surprises. Don't ever fucking do it again." Duke aggressively pushed the end call button even though it didn't have the same effect as his usual slamming of the landline phone.

With no real options and an impending tee time Duke walked to the conference room with earnest. Since this was a meeting to relay good news he knew it would go fast. He enjoyed seeing the look on people's faces when he told them that he personally selected them for a promotion.

"Ms. Cabrini please have a seat," said Duke as he swayed into the conference for perhaps the 20th and hopefully final time this week.

"It's Mrs. Cabrini but please call me Frankie." Frankie had been looking out the window admiring the view of the ducks on the pond on this Indian summer day. Sure beats the view of the corrugated boxes she sees most days.

"Well Frankie you're probably wondering why I asked to see you." He said while making eye contact for the first time.

"My supervisor said it was something about having me in mind for a promotion but he was not specific." questioned Frankie.

"Dammit," thought Duke, "I like to be the one to deliver good news. I have to remember to discuss this with Patrick."

"Yes. That's right. As you may have heard Gary has resigned and decided to pursue other interests."

Frankie interjected "Oh, everyone thinks he was fired for something because he was escorted out by security."

"No that's just a company policy and a formality…but the important point is that it means we have a new management opening. I believe you are the right person to take his place. The job pays 20% more than a grade 10. I understand you are a grade 8 now so that would be about a $12K raise." Duke paused waiting for the usual smile and thank you that typically followed. Instead Duke was staring at a poker face.

After a long pause Frankie said, "Thank you for considering me for the promotion. I'll talk it over with my husband tonight and give you an answer on Monday."

Duke thought, "What the fuck? No body has ever turned down a promotion by me. They have all jumped for joy."

Trying to put on his best poker face that was given up by the bulging and pulsing vein on his temple Duke replied, "That is a very good idea. Management can be very demanding and the job is not for everyone but this is a bit of a time sensitive nature. Let me propose that you start Monday as a temporary manager for two weeks. If you don't like it you go back to your old job."

"That seems fair but I still have to discuss it with my husband."

Duke was fuming internally. As calmly as he could he asked, "Could you discuss it with your husband tonight and call me on my cell phone tomorrow morning?"

"Yes, of course, but there is so much I don't know about the job. I have so many questions."

"Well why don't you spend some time with Sheila this afternoon and she can fill you in on the details. I have to run to an important offsite meeting and will be gone for the rest of the afternoon. Here's my cell number. I look forward to hearing positively from you tomorrow morning."

Duke stood up and Frankie took that as a queue that the meeting had ended. Without a goodbye Duke was already out the front door and heading toward his car parked in the reserved spot closest to the door. Frankie, still sitting at the conference room table was not sure what to make of the whole meeting but she got up and headed to HR.

"Hi Sheila!"

"Hi Frankie what brings you up here? Are you going to apply for that opening in customer service?"

"You mean you don't know why I'm here?"

"Nope."

Frankie and Sheila were not close friends but liked and respected each other. In fact, Sheila was the one who interviewed and hired Frankie 4 years ago.

Sheila felt like the mushroom woman – always kept in the dark and covered in shit by her boss. "Dammit Duke!" she thought.

"Duke told me I was being promoted to manager to replace Gary."

"What? Where's Gary? What's going on? I just got back from a doctor's appointment." This was par for the course but didn't make it any easier to accept. So frustrating not to find out about personnel decisions from her boss in a timely matter. He didn't understand that there were procedures to follow. Paperwork to fill out. Exit interviews to be discussed.

"Sheila, I don't know too much. All I can really tell you is what Duke has told me so far. And that's just that Gary resigned and he asked if I would fill his role. He said you would fill me in on the details."

"Frankie, can you give me a minute. Why don't you go back to the conference room and I will gather the management benefits materials and meet you there in five minutes."

"Of course." She said. She got up and closed the door. She thought this was the second time she had been dismissed from an office today. As she walked away she could hear Sheila yelling at Duke. She couldn't make out the words but she knew she was the topic.

3

"You're late. Did you miss the bus?" Joe asked.

"My day was great. Thanks for asking. How was your day, Joe?" Snapped Frankie.

"Sorry, let me start over. How was your day dear?"

"Awful. I don't want to talk about it now. We can talk about after the kids go to sleep. Where are they now? I want to see my babies." Frankie's voice and demeanor changed as soon as she mentioned her children. She had two healthy boys but secretly wanted a girl. Her favorite part of life was spending time with her kids. The only reason she went back to work was for a little extra money to help Joe pay to finish his college degree.

"Where do you think they are? They're not in here playing video games so the only other place is..."

"...out back playing basketball. Let's go challenge them to a game of two on two."

"So what made your day so awful? Heavy order day? A bunch of people call in sick the Friday before hunting season?" prodded Joe.

"Worse. They asked me to be a manager." Replied Frankie.

"Wow. When do you start?"

"What are you talking about? I didn't accept it. All I said is that I would discuss it with you and give Duke an answer in the morning. But there's nothing to discuss. I'm not taking the offer. It is chaos there. Besides I was only planning to work until you finished your degree and you are less than two semesters away. I want to be a stay-at-home mom again."

"That's fine, baby. I think it is an awesome that they recognized your skills and abilities. And even more awesome that you want to stay at home and take care of your three boys."

"Exactly. You are more work than the two of them put together...You know I almost accepted the job when they told me how much it pays. But then I thought of you and the kids and knew that the money was not important."

"Yeah, the moneys not important…but how much? Just tell me to satisfy my curiosity."

"Well what got my attention was not so much the money but the benefits that came with it. They match 100% of my 401K contributions. Medical insurance includes an HSA account and there's a performance bonus too."

"Wow that's a generous package. But how much were they going to pay you to…"

"…Sell my soul? Look we both agree it's not about the money when you finish your degree you can get that small business loan and start your own locksmith company. Then I'm back to work full time here." Interrupted Frankie.

"Yeah, you're right but just tell me how much?"

"Well if you include the 401K matching and the insurance, I would value the whole package at about $90K."

"$90K!!! Are you kidding me? Baby you're taking that job! Forget about my hopes and dreams. We're gonna be rich! Come here my sugar momma!"

"Mr. Regus, good morning. It's Frankie."

Duke was three strokes away from the best round of golf he'd played all summer. He quickly walked behind some shrubs because cell phones were discouraged on the greens and tee off areas.

He whispered, "Frankie, please, call me Duke. How did your discussion go with your husband?"

"Mr. Regus if I called you in the middle of something I can call you back later."

"FORE!" someone yelled in the distance as the sound of crunching branches startled him.

"No, no. Now's fine. What did you decide?" Duke replied as he bent over and picked up the ball that almost hit him and placed it in his pocket.

"Well we discussed the opportunity and decided to give it a try for two weeks like you suggested." Answered Frankie.

Perfect thought Duke. Just long enough to get that first paycheck then she'll be wearing the golden handcuffs.

"Great. Come to my office Monday at 1:30PM for the staff meeting and I will introduce you to the management team."

"OK but where should I go before that?"

"What do you mean where should you go before that?"

"Well Mr. Regus the shift starts at 7:30AM. I don't think I should show up on the first day unannounced to Gary's old crew."

"Oh no. You will not be managing Gary's old crew. You will be responsible for the packing area on second shift.

Didn't Sheila tell you? All new managers start on second shift. It's a little less stressful on-the-job training environment. And don't worry 2nd shift is only temporary. See you Monday at 1:30PM."

And the line went dead.

4

Monday morning came fast. Several years of habit forced Frankie to go to her locker. She was surprised to see her nameplate was already removed. The combination still worked so she opened it and placed her jacket and lunch inside.

Out of the corner of her eye she could see Sheila swiftly walking down the hall directly toward her carrying an armload of items.

"Hi Frankie, I've been trying to reach you all morning. We must not have your current phone number on file because your phone just rang and rang this morning."

"Oh that, I never answer my house phone. It always just telemarketers and I must not have given the company my cell phone number."

"Well here's your company cell phone. And it looks like you've already missed several calls and messages."

"What? Who even has this number?"

"You got me but that thing has been buzzing on my desk all morning. Here's your email address and login information. I have several documents you'll need to sign back at my desk…"

As Sheila rambled on about details Frankie quickly scanned the text messages. The first one read, "Staff meeting time changed to 12:00PM – working lunch." It was almost 1:30PM. She had to go, now.

"Then there's the medical insurance selection you must do before the end of open enrollment so start thinking about that now."

"Sheila, sorry, but I have to go. The staff meeting was moved to 12:00PM."

"What? I am on the staff too. No one told me!"

Both quickly made there way to the conference room. They stopped in front of the door and both took a deep breath and held it. Perhaps thinking that holding their breath would make them invisible long enough to find their seats at the conference room table.

Sheila and Frankie, being the only two women on the staff had all eyes on them as they made their way to the only two empty seats on either side of Duke.

"Ladies, welcome, please come sit down." beamed Duke, "Shelia I assumed you were off today. Did Linda forget to tell you about the meeting time change?"

"Yes, I just found out." Thinking that she would give Linda a piece of her mind when the staff meeting was over.

"No worries. Let's get back to business. Just to re-cap – Mike you'll host the client while they're here Tuesday and Patrick you will escort the client with Mike when they visit the shop floor. And if the client asks about Gary we tell them the truth he's on vacation this week. Any questions?"

"No? OK then on to the last item, which is not on our agenda – Frankie. As you all know I have chosen Frankie to fill in for the hole in our management team."

Frankie looked around the room and could feel the unspoken words. "Was this another diversity promotion?" Little did she and the other managers know but Duke didn't know her from Adam's off ox before she knocked on his office door.

The long stares would not penetrate her defensive shield. She would not be intimidated by a bunch of creepy ass crackers. She would prove her worth. She just wanted a little respect.

Duke asked her to give a brief history of her background so she did. When she finished she asked if there were any questions but no one did. The room fell silent. Clearly Duke was not listening. He was still trying to figure out how to conquer that water hazard on the number 4 hole that seems to swallow a golf ball every round.

"If there's nothing else Duke, I need to get back to the shop floor. I've been out nearly two hours and Mondays are always difficult with the backlog of orders that come in over the weekend. Not to mention the number of people who called in sick today." Said Patrick.

"Oh. No. Nothing else from my side. Does anyone else have something they would like to add or ask? No. Okay then meeting adjourned."

The sound of chairs being pushed in was cut by the gruffy voice of Wolf Bush. He was a manager whose reputation preceded him. He had curly, messy, salt and pepper hair. Tattoos of naked women on his forearms and what Frankie suspected was the scent of alcohol on his breath.

"Welcome to the jungle, Frankie. Let me give you the same advice I received when I was promoted. My boss said to me if I don't see your name written on the stalls of the bathroom wall then I'll assume you're not doing your job." Wolf belly laughed as he spoke that last line. He shook Frankie's hand and disappeared.

"Well Frankie that's Wolfie. He's quite the character but I'm sure you guys will get a long great. He's the picking manager and he'll be there to help mentor and guide you if you have questions."

"Oh my," thought Frankie, "That's my mentor?"

Sheila interjected, "Here's your crew roster. Your desk will be at the end of the packing line, Gary's old desk. I have to go have a word with Linda."

"Oh that won't be necessary I'll speak to her for you. You need to orient the new folks starting on second shift tonight." Said Duke.

Frankie made her way out of the office and out into the warehouse after picking up the documents in Sheila's office and placing them in her locker. She knew the path well having walked it for years. But she had never walked as far as the packing area. The whole time she worked there she had only worked in the picking aisles. She was surprised how far away it seemed.

As she walked along the conveyor belts she noticed a small box of packages marked with next day air labels. She looked at the shipping label and recognized it right away as an order she had picked at the end of her shift. "Why wasn't this on its way to the customers? Why weren't all these packages gone last Friday?" she asked herself.

There was no time to ponder the question any longer. She put the packages back where they were and walked to her desk. She turned on the computer and entered the email system for the first time. Her inbox showed 34 unread messages. "How can this be?" she thought to herself.

Before she could read any of the messages in her inbox she realized it was time for the shift to begin. It was time to introduce herself to her new crew. She felt excitement. The kind of feeling she had not had since her first day. "How would they react and respond?", she thought.

5

No one seemed to be listening to the speech she spent all weekend preparing. Even though it was the afternoon most of the crew looked like that had just rolled out of bed. Some sat on boxes. Most stood sipping coffee. But none seemed to really care what she had to say. It was a bit deflating.

She thanked them for their attention anyway, "And if you ever need any help from me I am here for you."

The crew dispersed to their packing workstations save one guy, Tim Combrero. He stood tall and thin with a few days stubble growth on his face. His brown hair was mostly covered by a Kodiak baseball hat. His brown eyes held up dark bags.

"Congratulations on your new job" complimented Tim. He slowly spit tobacco into a glass mug she wrongly suspected held coffee.

"Thank you, Tim." She replied and feeling obligated as a new manager she continued, "Please get rid of that mug before going to your station. I'm sure you know that tobacco use is not allowed on the line."

He laughed in response, "Don't worry. This is second shift. Besides I usually just swallow my spit."

The thought of swallowing tobacco saliva revolted her but she tried not to show it.

"Let me give you some advice to help you as a new manager. There are only three rules you need to follow: Number 1. Find out everyone's strengths and weaknesses."

"That sounds logical," she thought to herself.

"Number 2. Don't play favorites. And Number 3. Don't piss-off your people."

The second piece of advice seemed to make sense too. But was the third piece just a negative response to her mentioning the tobacco? She had full intention of following the first piece of advice. Right after she finished reading all her email.

Most of the messages were from Sheila. Some contained benefits information and some gave instructions on how to approve vacation and sick leave time in the labor management system. She was beginning to feel a bit overwhelmed by all the decisions she had to make and all the little administrative things she had to do each day.

The last email in her inbox was from Duke. It was addressed to the whole management team.

Dear Team,

As you are all aware MDG is coming tomorrow to review our corrective action plan. I cannot stress enough the importance of your cooperative behavior and rapid response to their questions during their visit.

MDG is a very important customer and the only reason we added 50K square feet to our warehouse. To maintain our margins and to ensure our longevity we need to keep MDG as a happy customer.

Sincerely,

Duke

"What does that mean? Is MDG threatening to leave? I know we have lost a few customers to the other 3PL's in the business park. Will MDG be the next?" Pondered Frankie.

6

Frankie went back to the box of expedited freight she saw at the beginning of the shift. It was still there! And now it was close to the end of shift. Where had the day gone? The last expedited freight trucks left hours ago.

"Cameron, do you know anything about these orders? Are they being held for any reason?" inquired Frankie.

"No ma'am. I don't know nothing about them boxes. They was here when I came in," he answered.

Being near the end of shift and with no one else to ask she decided to send a text message to her first shift counterpart and follow-up with an email with cc to Mike.

When she arrived home her husband was already in bed. He was awake and watching Sports Center. Before getting herself ready she went to check on her boys. Both were sound asleep with Gameboy still clutched in their hands. She went to the bathroom to check their toothbrushes – both were dry.

"How was your day?" he said with dollar signs in his eyes.

"Before we talk about my day. How was your evening? Did you check if the kids brushed their teeth? Did you make sure they weren't playing video games in bed? Let me answer for you. No you didn't! If I'm going to be working second shift you are going to need to be responsible for taking care of them in the evening."

"Sorry, let me start over. How was your evening my beautiful wife?" he said a little sheepishly.

"My evening?...I don't know...I mean I was running from the moment I got there until the moment I left...and I'm not sure what I accomplished."

"I got there early only to find out I was late for the first staff meeting. That was embarrassing. But not too bad because Sheila was also late."

"When I got there Sheila hands me my cell phone and I got a bunch of missed calls and text messages. The first one I read says staff meeting moved to noon. I can't believe I was an hour and a half late for my first meeting."

"After the meeting that strange manager I told you about before, Wolf Bush, the one with the naked ladies tattooed on his forearms, he told me I'm not doing my job unless I see my name written on the bathroom wall? Other than that no one said a word to me. In fact if I hadn't been late I don't think anyone would have noticed I was there.

"Before the shift started I found expedited freight packages I had picked last week just sitting under the conveyor belt and no one knew why they were there or even seemed to care." Frankie's pace continued to increase.

"Then that speech I worked on all weekend to introduce myself to my crew had about the same reaction as when I practiced it in front of the mirror."

"I don't know if anyone heard a thing I said. It was like I was talking to zombies. One guy was chewing tobacco and spitting it into a clear glass mug. It was disgusting. I thought I was going to throw up. Although I have to say he is one of my best workers. His packs per hour were higher than anyone else in my department."

"After the crew got started I opened my email to find 34 messages. As I started reading them the conveyor belt broke down so we had to manually transfer packages with carts until maintenance could fix it.

"Whoa...slow down. Take a breath. Sounds like you were running around like a chicken with your head cut off," said Joe. "It reminds me of the time I coached our son's soccer team when he was 4 years old. Remember that? Twenty-two kids chasing after the soccer ball but no one focusing on the goal."

"That's what it was like. I was running around chasing soccer ball fires. Tomorrow it's probably going to be worse because we are expecting a visit from our client. Apparently they are upset with our backlog and several shipping errors we have made. And I can't help but wonder if that box I found is one of those errors. I mean, how does a box of expedited freight go unnoticed?"

"Well the packing area is new to you. You spent all your time in picking so you know that well. You need to take sometime to understand the system from picking through packing. Take some time to map the whole system so you can understand it before you try to solve one-off problems. Remember that rich old lady who lived alone in that great big house in the country? I always got the call because no one liked driving out there and she had a bunch of dogs."

"Of course, she was one of your best customers. What happened to her?"

"Well in hindsight I was just fixing single problems. She was forever losing keys to the various doors in her house. So I would go there, re-key the cylinder and give her a new key with a big keychain thinking she would not lose it. But she would still keep losing the keys. Well about the third trip out there I saw where she kept her keys in a big drawer. There was a sea of keys. I recognized a few of the key chains I had given her. I realized she wasn't really losing the keys at all. She was just forgetting which key fit which lock. So I suggested that I could label each key with which door it opened or I could change all the lock cylinders so they work with one single key. Since money was no object to her she went for the single key solution and I haven't seen her since. So the point is to make sure you understand the whole system before you try to solve the problem and never forget the goal."

"Never forget the goal? What's that supposed to mean?"

"I'm not sure yet. I was hoping you would know. My first correspondence class in operations management was tonight. The professor started out the class calmly asking each person what the goal was. He went around the room asking each individual. People answered variations of 'to make money' and 'to make a profit'. The further it went along the louder he got asking the question. It was intimidating enough watching on my computer. I cannot imagine being there in person. Anyway he said we all failed to answer the question correctly. He would not tell us the answer. And unless we figured it out we would all fail the class."

"Your teacher sounds strange."

7

"Are they here yet?" Duke asked.

"Nope. I've been watching the parking lot. They're definitely not here yet." Answered Mike.

Duke was pacing the conference room like a caged lion. "Dammit, where can they be? Their flight landed five hours ago."

"Why don't you just call, Duke?"

"And sound like I'm desperate? No way. You call. No better yet ask Linda to call."

The conference room door opened and in walked Linda with a stern look on her face. Without salutation, "Just got a phone call from MDG. They are running a bit late at another meeting and will come by after lunch. And when you have a minute we need to talk about a conversation I just had with Sheila about forgetting to copy her on the notification of the staff meeting time change." The door closed.

"Whom could they be meeting with? Oh no, do you think they are meeting with our rival Maltese?"

"Duke, relax. Why are you so paranoid? They wouldn't switch 3PL's so soon after signing a contract with us unless we are really screwing up and besides we have a termination clause in our contract that they have to give us plenty of notice and I never once heard them mention that to us. Even after we missed those strategic orders last week. They are probably just meeting with a supplier."

Duke was not going to mention that he had heard them use the termination clause in the last conference call. "Mike, its an arbitrage business model. Their suppliers are in Asia; their manufacturing is in Asia. The only thing they have here is distribution and that's us. God damn it! They're switching to our competitor."

"Hang on, this is Chicago. They have plenty of customers around here. Could they be talking to one of them? Remember that big order we missed last week? That was for McDonald's and they're only a half hour away. Maybe they are talking with them?" That's what Duke liked about Mike. He was always a voice of reason and he was loyal like a dog. No matter how often Duke kicked him in the ass.

Duke thought he would take him with him on his next assignment at corporate or to that new facility they were talking about building in Georgia. "Just to be safe go over to Maltese. Put on a pair of work boots, a Cubs hat and lose the collared shirt. Walk in there and say you're there to fill out an application. When the security guard goes to get you an application look at the visitor log and see if you see anyone from MDG."

"Alright. I'll go check it out but I think you're being paranoid."

Being the good soldier Mike followed orders. He went to the lost and found. There he grabbed the cleanest looking t-shirt in his size, the only size 13 boots and a Sox hat. He thought, "I hope nobody sees me in this Sox hat. I hate those guys." The cross-town series was this week and he was hoping Duke would offer the company's seats to him so he could take his son.

After getting in his car Mike noticed that although the shirt looked clean it smelled like sweat. He had to roll down the windows to stave off the gag reflex. The short ride was a welcome break from the stresses in the office. The Enya CD he was listening to dropped his blood pressure a few digits. Driving alone in your car is one of the last freedoms left. Enya and the serenity of the drive were interrupted by call coming over his blue tooth.

Mike knew who it was immediately. "Well? What's the status Gladys?" Mike hated that he always called him Gladys when he asked for the status.

"Duke I'm just pulling into the drive way." He snapped.

"What? What's taking so long? You left an hour ago." Duke snapped back.

"Duke I left ten minutes ago. I had to search the lost and found to find some clothes that fit and didn't look like I slept in them. I'm just about up to the visitor parking area...wait a minute...oh my god. They're here. I'm coming back."

"No wait. Go in anyway. After they leave. Stick to the plan. But look at the times of their entries on the visitor log. The longer they were there the worse it is for us."

"Okay."

From the vantage point of the employee parking lot Mike observed closely as the Maltese's management team walked them to their rental car. They were all handshakes and smiling

43

faces. This did not look good. After they drove away Mike made his way to the visitor lobby to execute the plan.

"What can I do for you?" the no-nonsense guard asked.

"Good afternoon. I'd like to apply for a job."

"We don't accept unsolicited applications. Everyone we hire needs to be referred by an existing employee."

Mike was quick on his feet. Another quality Duke abused. "Oh, yes. Gary Madowski referred me. He's a manager here."

"I don't know a Gary Madowski. I thought I knew all the managers."

"He actually just started."

"Let me check the directory. M-A-D? Oh yes. Here it is. He just started yesterday. No wonder I don't know him. Okay just a minute I'll get you an application and then page him for you."

"Oh that's not necessary I don't want to disturb him. I just want to fill out the application."

"Well it's company policy. He needs to receive the application from you and hand it into HR. Just sign in to the visitor log, have a seat and I will be right back."

Mike pretended to sign into the visitor log while quickly scanning the names. He had no intention of waiting for the guard to return with an application and the manager who once reported to him.

There they were. All four names from MDG, first thing this morning. No wait. The date says yesterday. They were here all day yesterday and today. "That can't be a good sign," thought Mike.

The news was unnerving to Duke. He struggled with what he should do with the information. Only he and Mike knew they were talking to the competitor. So he should be able to keep a lid on this can of worms. Should he tell the owners what he knew? There was really only one quarter left before he would get his performance bonus. His EBITDA numbers were there but if the owners found out about the possibility of losing MDG that would not fare well with the discretionary portion of his bonus. He decided to keep quiet for the time being.

Duke met Mike in the parking lot. "Mike get out of those old clothes and meet me in the conference room. We need to strategize a plan before MDG gets here. Don't say anything to anyone about what you just saw. We can fix this so no one has to know. We probably have about a half hour, 60 minutes tops before they arrive."

"Too late. That's their rental car parked in the visitor spot." They must have walked into the main lobby as Duke walked out the employee entrance.

"Holy crap! Are you sure? Quick. Go change and I'll stall

them in the conference room."

"Gentlemen…and lady. Great to see you guys again in Chicago. You know we just happen to have four tickets to tonight's cross town series at Wrigley Field if you're interested." Offered Duke.

"Thanks Duke but we are leaving later tonight. We're a little pressed for time so if you don't mind we'd like to get started." Replied Reuben.

"No problem. I understand. Let me call Mike and Patrick in here. They prepared a presentation which describes our corrective action plan as well as our rate readiness plan for the expected increase in volumes in the first quarter."

"With all do respect Duke we would prefer just a tour of our packing area and the returns & exchanges area."

"Oh shit!" thought Duke, "I am fucked. These guys aren't fooling around any more."

A ruffled Mike walked in the conference room with an anxious looking Patrick right behind him.

"Perfect timing boys," said Duke, "I was just about to take Reuben and his team on a tour of the packing line and the returns area. Patrick why don't you lead the way. Just in time for second shift to start."

"Gary's on vacation this week so Patrick will lead the tour," said Mike.

"Mike, according to Gary's LinkedIn page he is working at Maltese now." Reuben corrected.

"Oh," a reddened Mike said, "He's hunting this week and then he's leaving." Duke wanted to slap him.

As they walked back to the MDG packing area a nervous Patrick tried to describe their newly implemented inspection process over the sound of the pulsing conveyor belts and the sounding horns of the fork trucks. Reuben drifted back looking at a box that caught his eye.

"Duke, why is this box of expedited freight sitting here? These packages are marked from last week." Inquired Reuben.

"They're probably just waiting for an out of stock item before they all ship."

"All these packages are labeled. Duke, I've seen enough. We're sending in auditors to ensure our customers are cared for."

8

"Let's go. Hurry or you guys are going to miss your bus." Yelled Frankie. "And if you miss the bus, I'm not driving you."

It didn't seem to matter how early she got her kids up for school. They were always rushing to make the bus. They were no doubt playing some video game in their room.

Her boys ran down the stairs and were out the door in a flash. It was only 7:30AM and she had nothing else to do until work. What should she do with her morning?

She plopped on the couch and started flipping channels. She became mesmerized watching a white guy with an Afro and beard paint a mountain landscape. As she was hypnotized by the paintbrush strokes and his soothing voice she drifted back to that confrontation she had last night with Duke.

"Why are these packages sitting here?" Duke said without even saying hello to her. She could tell by his body language that he was agitated about something.

"Mr. Regus I saw these packages last night…"

"What," Duke interrupted, "These have been here since last night. Why didn't you do something about them?"

"Well, actually they have been there since Friday afternoon because if you see here on the pick sheet these are my initials. I picked this order Friday morning sometime. When I noticed them last night I asked around and no one knew what was going on. So I sent a note to my counter part on first shift and cc'd Mike."

"Mike come with me. Frankie I don't ever want to see expedite freight packages delayed again." Commanded Duke.

Frankie felt like she was going to cry. How was she supposed to know what to do? No one really gave her any expectations.

Just then Wolf walked up. "Hey don't take it personal. Duke's an asshole. He was just looking for a scape goat and you were the nearest lamb to slaughter."

"How do you put up with him?" asked Frankie.

"Well I avoid him. That's one of the reasons I love second shift. If I plan my doctor's appointments, dental appointments and vacation days right I hardly see the man."

Frankie felt some relief. "Avoidance, well thanks for your advice. But that won't be so easy for me because this is just temporary. I'm only on second shift temporarily."

Wolf belly laughed, "Is that what he told you? Second shift would be temporary? Let me ask you a question. You've been here long enough. How many time have you seen manager switch shifts?"

She snapped back to the reality of lying on her couch by the sound of the ringing house phone. She was too comfortable to get up to answer. She made a mental note to discuss with Joe the possibility of second shift being a little longer than just this semester.

She lay on the couch staring at the ceiling trying to figure out how there were marks on her ceiling. Boys were easier than girls but they sure make a mess. She thought how nice it was to wake her kids up and make them breakfast and get them ready for school. Second shift wasn't so bad in the morning.

She couldn't sit still any longer. She decided to catch up on laundry when she heard the phone ring. Of course the basement phone wasn't in its cradle and she was not about to run up stairs for what was likely a telemarketer anyway. She continued sorting whites from darks and made a mental note to check with her sons to see if they were wiping themselves after using the bathroom.

She heard the phone ring again. It was like the seductive sounds of the sirens. She could not resist. She ran up the basement stairs as fast as she could but as soon as she grabbed the kitchen phone the line went dead.

As soon as she placed it back it the receiver it rang again. "Hello?"

"Hi baby. It's your favorite husband. Hey I was thinking since you're home and I'm in the neighborhood maybe I could come home for lunch. What do you think?"

"Oh that would be so nice to have lunch quietly together. So romantic."

Joe thought to himself, "Well that's not exactly my idea of romance. What I meant was I wanted to come home for a nooner." The other lined beeped interrupting their call.

"Baby, let me get this other call. I'll see you for lunch but come early because I want to get to work by 2PM."

She clicked over but again was too late. She checked the caller ID and saw it was a number from work. Just then her work cell phone started vibrating on the kitchen counter.

"Hello?"

"Frankie, this is Sheila. We had an accident in the warehouse. Can you come into work right now?"

"Sure. What happened?"

"Just hurry. A picker died." Click.

9

She drove on autopilot. She was holding on to the steering wheel and pressing the gas pedal but only habit was guiding her to the warehouse. Traffic was still heavy from the morning rush commute, which was disrupted by the unseasonal drizzle.

The only sound she heard was the sound of her windshield wipers going back and forth and the chatter as it scraped across the windshield. It was not raining hard enough to keep her wipers on constantly but she was tired of turning them on and off again.

She knew exactly how someone died. She didn't need to hear it from anyone. She knew. The question that split her head was who? She cried all the way to work just thinking about it.

She turned into the parking lot and was greeted by an ambulance, a fire truck and the coroner's wagon that blocked the management parking stalls. She found a spot in the back of the lot and tried to keep from getting too wet as she shuffled to the entrance. Just then they wheeled out a body covered with a white sheet. She started to cry again.

Sheila met her at the door. Frankie regained her composure and since it was raining probably no one could tell she was crying. The only word she could muster was, "Who?"

Sheila responded, "Arturo Caballero."

Frankie was relieved that it was no one she knew personally but still saddened by the loss.

"We just hired him from the temp agency. Hell, I was just processing his paperwork this morning. I need your help. You need to call his family."

"Sheila, I can't. What would I say? I'm not good at these kinds of things."

"No you have to. I checked the database and you're the only manager who speaks Spanish. When I called the family this morning whoever answered did not speak any English. The family needs to know. I'll help you with the words you just have to do the talking."

After the most painful call of her life she was summoned to Duke's office. He looked more disturbed and annoyed than distraught. In his typical command and control style he said, "Frankie, it's a tragedy what happened out there. OSHA is going to be here any minute and I need you to be their guide during their accident investigation."

"Yes, sir, anything I can do to help."

The OSHA investigator took notes as Frankie described the picking process. He didn't so much write words as he drew pictures.

"Excuse me but could I get a copy of your report before you go."

"No I cannot give you my notes only the report when it is finalized. What I can tell you is that this accident was typical of what we see all the time. It was textbook and preventable. Most accidents occur at the beginning or end of a shift. This one happened right at the beginning. Most fatalities are falls just like this one. And last, most accidents are the result of the behavior and decisions of the individual."

"Oh, I understand. Well it's not really your notes I'm interested in. I like how you mapped the process."

"Well I can give you one of our blank forms. Would that be helpful?"

"Yes it would. Thank you."

"Thank you, Frankie, you have been very helpful. I don't think I need anything else right now but can I get your business card if I think of something else?"

"Oh I don't have any business cards. Give me one of yours and I will send you a message with my contact details."

Frankie felt funny having a conversation with someone just a few feet from where someone died. As they spoke the biohazard contractors where moping up blood and God knows what else. "Thanks again for your help. Could you direct me to the Human Resources manager's office? I would like to see your safety protocols and job descriptions. And then I'll be on my way."

"Sure."

It was just past 1PM. Frankie just realized that she was supposed to meet Joe for lunch. She called immediately.

"Able Locksmith. This is Joe."

"Joe. It's me. Sorry I forgot about lunch." She whispered.

"Yeah, what the hell? And what number are you calling me from? I tried calling your cell and it went straight to voicemail. And why are you whispering?"

"Sorry," she hushed. "I can't really talk right now. I'm at work standing outside Duke's office. There was a fatality accident so I had to go in early. This is my work cell phone I must have forgotten to give you the number. I think I may have left my personal cell phone at home because I left in such a rush this morning. I'm sorry. I can't talk right now. I've got to report to Duke what the OSHA investigator asked me. I'll see you tonight. Bye."

As she knocked on the door to Duke's office she was startled by the loud response, "Please come in Frankie and tell your husband I said hello."

Duke was standing behind her the whole time.

10

After briefing Duke and Mike on the OSHA investigation she got her crew started and got through with the administrative tasks as quickly as possible. She didn't bother to check her email because she did not want to see what was waiting for her.

The early morning tragedy lay heavily on the hearts and minds of those on second shift. It could have been anyone of them. The somber atmosphere was too much for Frankie. She needed to collect her thoughts and refresh her mind. But where to go? What to do? The shift just started.

The fall in temperature today had already penetrated the thin walls of the warehouse. It felt cold and damp and smelled like a basement. She went to her locker to get her sweater. Frankie then found the quietest place in the warehouse and took seat. The cold toilet seat startled her. Her eyes opened wide when she saw her name written on the back of the stall wall door. 'Frankie is a kiss ass' was written just beneath a sketch of a woman kissing the big ass of a man. It was too much for one day. She cried as quietly as possible.

After a few minutes she gained her composure, checked her make-up and made her way back to the packing area. She decided to use the form she got from the OSHA investigator to map out the packing process in an effort to understand how the expedited freight problem occurred.

"Excuse me, Cameron, can you explain to me how you manage the expedited freight every day."

"Yes, ma'am. It's really quite simple. In fact the process really doesn't change much no matter what type of package it is. When the boxes comes down the conveyor belt I look at the shipping label and then put it on the pallet for that shipper."

"Thank you. Now I can see pallets for each of the different carriers but I don't see one for expedited freight."

"Yes, ma'am. I usually don't see much expedited freight so I move that pallet out of the way so I have more room. It's gone now so someone must have taken it to the dock."

"Who moves that pallet to the dock?"

"I'm not sure ma'am. It usually goes away before I go to lunch."

"Thanks Cameron. I'll wander over to the dock and ask around. I want you to do me a favor if you ever see expedited freight packages still sitting here before you leave for lunch I want you to notify me or another manager."

"Yes ma'am."

The lunch bell sounded and everyone disappeared. Frankie found herself looking down a conveyor belt devoid of people but full of boxes. The smell of tobacco smoke filled the air and Wolf appeared.

"Hey Frankie. How's it going?"

"Hi Wolf. I wish I could say good."

"I know. What a terrible day. Young kid with a family. What a tragedy. Whatcha working on there?"

"Oh I'm just trying to understand the packing process and while I'm at it make sure expedited freight packages are never missed again."

"Just a suggestion, we used to flow out processes using craft paper and the actual documents. The college boys called it a brown paper process mapping. For example, take those missed orders Duke was blaming on you yesterday. Just print out duplicate picking, packing and shipping labels. That way you will have a very specific paper trail example with actual documents showing where the failures in the processes occurred and at the same time you will be able to visualize the whole system."

"Huh…maybe I misjudged Wolf," she thought, "He's not such a bad guy after all."

"Good idea, Wolf. I'll try that. Thanks."

The process took a lot longer than she expected. Partly because she had to fit it in between crises. Each time she finished a part of the process she would check her work with Wolf, some of the other supervisors and leads. By the end of the second week she had a document 20 feet long filled with actual documents that showed the system flow as it was.

What was clear about the expedited freight process is that no one was really in charge or responsible for making sure the last pallet made it on the 7PM truck. Luckily she had resolved that problem by making it Cameron's responsibility. There hadn't been a single missed expedited package since.

She also observed there were no feedback loops between the adjacent processes. Once an order was picked it was thrown over the fence to the packing department. And when packing finished their work they threw the order over the fence to the shipping department. When she looked at the error rates in each department she was amazed anything got done right. Each department was reporting about a 95% quality rate, which individually may meet customer requirements, but since it's a system the real quality rate is the product of the system (95% x 95% x 95%) or 85%!

She rolled up her brown paper. Proud of her work she decided she would save it as a training tool for new hires and temporary workers. With absenteeism running 10% there were temps almost nightly and with turnover close to 30% she could see using the document regularly.

Frankie couldn't believe almost two weeks had passed. She had decided by the end of the first week that she enjoyed the work enough to make the change permanent but she still wanted to talk it over with her husband. Duke had been pressing her all week for an answer about making the move permanent but every time she asked him about how long she would be on second shift he was elusive. He at least treated her better since the expedited freight problems went away. She told him she would give him an answer by next Monday and in the event her decision was no she would finish out the week so they could find a replacement.

Friday morning of the second week Frankie woke up in a good mood. She felt a little more in control of her new roles and responsibilities. She loved waking up with her kids and getting them ready for school. Even though it was the same struggle every day to get them on the bus in time.

She got into a routine of doing housework once the kids were out the door. That was followed by 30 minutes on the stair master that had really only served as a clothing rack since she'd bought it. She was feeling good about herself and her job but a little guilty about her relationship with her husband. He was usually asleep by the time she got home so other than breakfast they hardly had time for each other during the week. She decided to call him to see if they could meet for lunch.

"Able Locksmith. This is Joe."

"Hey my husband is at work. Do you want to come over for a nooner?"

11

Having had his idea of a romantic lunch with his wife, Joe decided that would be the start of a great weekend. He decided to take the rest of the afternoon off. After parking his truck in the garage he wandered down the driveway to pick up the mail: junk, bills, more junk, People magazine and…... Frankie's paycheck.

"Hmmm," he thought to himself, "I wonder how much it is. Frankie wouldn't mind if I opened it. Or would she? She always said not to open her mail and that if I did it was a federal offense and she would have me arrested. But is it really if were married? Oh it doesn't matter she would kill me anyway. Maybe I could just steam open the envelope enough to peek inside and then seal it back up?"

Joe waited impatiently for the tea kettle to start to boil. He stood above the stove with the envelope in hand. He had never done this before but he remembered reading about it in a book once. Finally steam began to pour through the top. He waved the back of the envelop over the stream of steam while the kettle released a high pitch whistle. His hands couldn't take more heat. Now was the time to try opening it.

He slowly and carefully began to peel back the flap. He didn't get very far before it tore.

"Dammit. Now what I am going to do. That won't work…Wait I can check the bank balance on-line…crap Frankie does all that and there's no way I'll remember the password…I know…I can go check the balance with my ATM card."

Joe decided he would justify the trip by also picking his kids up from school. He pulled into the Chase parking lot and ran inside to check his account balance. Being a Friday there was a short line. He waited his turn. Inserted his card and hit the balance request. When he saw the digits on the screen his mouth dropped and his eyes widened. He obviously stood motionless too long because the guy behind him in line asked if there was a problem with the machine.

Frankie came home to find her husband had waited up for her. There were scented candles glowing in the family room and a bouquet of flowers on the table.

"To what do I owe this pleasure?"

"Oh wait there's more. I have a special surprise. Sit down I have something I want to show you." He slipped a CD into the DVD player.

"Oh my god! Did you tape our lunch date without me knowing? You are dead Mr. Cabrini!"

"No, no, no. I wish. Good idea. I'll tape it next time."

"Oh there won't be a next time if you try that."

The DVD began playing her son's first basketball game. A tear streamed down her face as she realized she had missed another milestone in her son's life because of work. She had completely forgotten that is was this week.

"Thank you for recording this," she cried.

They watched the game in silence. Frankie smiled every time her son touched the ball. She didn't even notice or care that her son's team lost by more than 20 points.

After the game was over Frankie turned to her husband and said we need to talk. Joe knew those words were the precursor to a conversation he would rather not have.

He put on his game face and said, "Sure. What's up?"

"It's about my job. I like it but I don't want to miss our kids growing up. I'm going tell Duke on Monday that I want to go back to my old job."

"Baby don't be rash with your decision. Duke told you himself that second shift was only temporary. You won't miss our kids growing up. Besides have you seen your paycheck yet?"

"I don't need to see my paycheck. It's not about the money. I'm telling Duke Monday that I'm done."

He could tell by her tone that arguing was pointless.

12

"I need to go to second shift immediately," declared Bill.

Duke hated dealing with these personnel issues. That was why he had Patrick and Mike. They were supposed to be a line of defense to handle all of these trivial people problems.

"Bill, did you speak with Patrick?"

"I don't have time to ask Patrick or Mike only to have them say they can't make a decision without asking you and then wait for the HR paperwork. I need to go to second shift now. You need to transfer me today."

Duke didn't care to have anyone tell him what he needed to do. But even he could sense that there was something wrong.

"Bill what's wrong? Why do you need to go to second shift so desperately?"

"It's my wife. She is sick and I need to be available to take her to her chemo treatments during the day."

"Oh Bill, I'm sorry to hear that. But it's not as simple as me approving your request. I need to find someone who will come to first shift."

"Duke I haven't taken a vacation day in years. I have accrued over 12 weeks, which with holidays coming up would take me into next year sometime. It's also coincidently exactly the amount of time the Family Leave Medical Act will allow me to take without jeopardizing my job. So I will see you in January or when you find someone who will switch with me."

Duke could not believe his Monday. It wasn't even 8 o'clock and he already felt like he was put through the ringer. He read in the local paper that the company was being sued for negligence for the recent fatality accident. Then when he arrived at work he had a message from the corporate attorney that the company was being sued for failing to pay the 10% construction holdback to the general contractor for the site expansion. To make matters worse he was personally being named in the suit. The last thing he needed was dealing with these personnel issues.

"Mr. Regus, Frankie is here to see you," said Linda.

"Sure. Send her in," replied Duke. Finally some good news he thought. "No one would come tell me in person that they were quitting a management position. They would send me an email or leave a message with Linda."

"Good afternoon Mr. Regus."

"Good afternoon Frankie. How many times do I have to tell you to call me Duke?"

"Sorry sir. I just wanted to speak with you face to face. You asked me to give you an answer about making this a permanent change. I spoke to my husband…"

Duke thought, "I'm sure she saw her paycheck stub by now and can't wait for the next one. Here it comes…"

"And we decided that it was best for our family for me to go back to my old job. I'll finish out this week so you can find someone to take my place. Or if you already have someone in mind I can go back as soon as possible."

"Contain your anger Duke," he tried to coach himself.

"Why did you decide that? What didn't appeal to you?" asked Duke.

"Well the work was rewarding – high highs but also low lows. The…"

"What if I gave you a 10% raise? Would it change your mind?"

"No, the…"

"15% but that's the best I can do."

"Thank you, Duke, but it's not about the money. It just that second shift is taking a toll on me personally. I know you said it was temporary but I just can't wait for whenever that will be."

"Dammit," Duke thought to himself, "I just paid for something I could have gotten for free."

"I'll tell you what, Frankie, I like you and I don't want second shift to be the reason you give up this career opportunity. What if I said you could start on first shift tomorrow? Would that change your mind?" offered Duke.

"Well…let me talk it over with Joe and see what he thinks. I'll get back to you tomorrow morning."

"Thanks, Frankie. Either way come in on first shift tomorrow. " Duke managed to say politely but he was seething inside as he thought to himself, "The correct answer was an emphatic YES!"

13

"I can't believe you would wake me to ask me something so ridiculous." Joe was upset to be woken from a deep sleep. "They're going to put you on first shift starting tomorrow and give you a 15% raise? What's there to talk about?" As he rolled over and went back to sleep.

"Well that's what I thought but I wanted to get your input." Responded Frankie.

"It felt nice to be on first shift again but strange at the same time," thought Frankie. Now she would be managing some of the same people she used to work with when she was a picker. The picking area was her comfort zone the only trepidation she felt was being in the management role.

The start of shift went smoothly except for the fact that five employees hadn't shown up for work. There was no way she was going to make her productivity numbers being so short handed. She could get a few temps on short notice but who would teach them what to do? Before she could make a decision about bringing in temps she received a text message indicating an all managers meeting to discuss the follow-up response to OSHA.

Mike, Patrick, Sheila, Frankie and John sparsely populated the main conference room. The meeting was supposed to begin 10 minutes ago but they were still missing several of the area managers yet Mike decided to get going any way.

"Guys I don't know where everyone else is but we need to get this out to legal today for approval so we can send it to OSHA by Friday," began Mike. "The explanation we need to provide is how we are going to prevent this from happening again in the future. They provided this Root Cause Analysis form for us to fill out. I thought rather than try to do this in a vacuum I would get your inputs."

Patrick handed out copies so everyone could look at the same form. The form had the problem statement in the upper left corner of the landscape document. Underneath and slightly to the right were three boxes evenly spaced to the bottom of the page. To the right of each of these boxes were four more boxes evenly spaced to the other edge of the document. A line connected each row of boxes and in between each box was the question Why.

The purpose was to understand what happened; why it wasn't detected before it happened and how do we ensure it never happens again.

"Now I hate this bullshit regulation as much as you do. I think if we work together we can get this pencil-whipped in no time," said Mike. "Now why do you guys think this happened?"

"He shouldn't have been up there in the first place," said John. He was clearly trying to shift blame to the individual and away from him, the manager who's employee died in an industrial accident.

"That's not the point. Why did this happen? Why did someone fall in our warehouse?" Sheila brought the focus back to the event and not the person. "We have safety procedures, briefings, training and PPE. This should not have happened."

"Did Arturo go through the safety orientation before he started?" asked Patrick.

"Yes, of course, he went through the new employee safety orientation training. But I don't believe he had fall protection training. Usually only the stockers and sometimes maintenance get that training because they're typically the only ones working on the high racks or conveyors." Explained John.

"Let's try using this Five Why form." Interjected Mike bringing the group back to the Root Cause Analysis document. "Why did he fall?"

"He wasn't wearing a harness." Suggested Patrick.

"No he was wearing a harness but he never tied on." Corrected John.

"Good," thought Mike. "That will be in our favor for the lawsuit. It was not the company's fault. We provided the equipment. It was his behavior. He chose not to tie on."

"OK the first answer to the question why did he fall was that he did not tie on. Why didn't he tie on?" asked Sheila.

"I guess because the only tie on points are near where the maintenance guys are changing out motors or the belt itself. If he had tied on there he would not have been able to reach the box jam which was usually occurs ten feet or more from those points." Responded John.

Frankie listened patiently. She was still unsure of herself and her ability to add to the conversation.

"So he didn't tie on because there was not a point close to where he was working." Mike thought from a legal perspective that is not in our favor.

Patrick added, "He could have used a snorkel lift and tied on to that."

Frankie thought to herself that was the most ridiculous thing she had ever heard. There is no way that would ever happen. She began filling out the document herself to see where it led her.

"Good. He didn't tie on because he didn't use a snorkel lift. Why didn't he use a snorkel lift?"

"Probably because there is only one and maintenance is using it 100% of the time right now as they change out the HID lights to those more cost effective ones."

"Well that takes us to the 5th why. So what are we going to do about these issues to make sure that it never happens again?"

"Sounds like our corrective action is to put in an CapEx request for a second snorkel lift which will never be approved and if it does it will take 12 months or more. So maybe for the interim we can look at procuring longer tethers for our harnesses and put in a request for maintenance to weld more tie-on points along the upper conveyor. Those can be done quickly and should satisfy OSHA."

"The other important element is behavioral. We provided everything the employee needed to work safely and still he chose not to."

Frankie began stewing in her chair. This is always the corrective action: spend more on capital and train the employee to correct their behavior. This was wrong and she knew it. She could not contain herself.

"BULLSHIT!" she screamed. Everyone turned to look at her.

"Excuse me," regaining her composure, "but I think we are going down the wrong path. When I ask the question why did Arturo fall I know it's because he lost his balance when the conveyor started back up.

Why did he lose his balance? He was clearing boxes that had jammed up. The conveyor stops automatically when there is a certain level of resistance and then restarts when the resistance is removed.

Why was he clearing a jam? We have jams at the start of most shifts.

Why do we have jams at the beginning of the shift? Pickers start before the packers. Until the packers start their line the boxes just accumulate sometimes to the point of jamming up.

Why do pickers start before packers? Because the previous packing shift empties the conveyor belt of all boxes and totes in the system. Since we don't want to pay for the packers to stand around and wait for the pickers to send totes down the line we stagger their start by an hour. So in my opinion the root cause of this tragedy is our management policy to stagger the shifts and dry the lines at the end of each shift.

And now that I think about it I bet this is the reason we got so many picking errors at the beginning of each shift. When the belt jams, totes tip over and packages get mixed together."

No one could dispute her logic or challenged her conclusions. Mike broke the awkward silence that followed. "Well I like the corrective action of changing our policy better than spending money on a new snorkel lift."

Patrick thought, "That's not going to look good on our response to OSHA and certainly not in court."

"I guess that brings us to the corrective action. What should we do about this? If I remember right we staggered the shifts so that there would not be such a queue waiting to go out through the metal detectors and so there would be parking spaces available. If we go back to the old policy we would eliminate one problem but create another."

"What if we just tweak that policy by shortening the time between shifts and eliminating the drying of the packing lines," suggested John. "That should eliminate the beginning of shift jams and reduce some of overtime we were paying to get the lines completely empty."

"That's a win-win. We'll start that ASAP. Patrick send out a memo to all your managers announcing the new policy that starts immediately." Mike ordered.

14

Frankie was surprised by how long it took for that meeting. But she felt good because she believed they came to the right conclusion. She glanced at the time to see they had debated all through lunch. She walked back to her area but found no one.

"Where is everyone? Lunch ended five minutes ago." Frankie said to herself. She felt as though the people she used to work with were taking advantage of her. Just as she was about to call Sheila to ask for advice her crew began returning one by one.

She quickly checked her packages picked per person per hour. They were actually on target yet they were down 5 people. She looked closer at the details to see there were several large full case orders that inflated her numbers. It was just the break she needed.

She walked back to Sheila's office for advice on how to handle the issue of people returning late from lunch. Sheila greeted her with a big hug.

"Thank you for being in that meeting, Frankie. You really made a difference. You don't know how many of those I have sat through and the conclusion is all the same. I have stacks of these accident investigation forms and they all blame the employee for their behavior and recommend buying more of something to reduce the chances of the accident happening again. And the best part is when you yelled bullshit. Did you see their faces?!"

Slightly embarrassed Frankie responded, "I'm sorry I just couldn't help myself. It just seemed so far off the mark where they were going."

"Don't apologize. You were right. I finally feel like we came to a true root cause and this will never happen again."

"Thanks. But I came to talk to you about a different problem I have with my crew. When I came back from the meeting there was no one there. Lunch had ended over 5 minutes ago. I didn't say anything when they returned because I saw we were making our numbers but I feel I should say something when I start the crew tomorrow. What should I say, Sheila?"

"Frankie that is a classic problem. The biggest obstacle you have to correcting it is the fact that no two managers here address this problem the same way. We have a progressive discipline system here, which you are no doubt aware of but it is only used for one thing: absences. We have close to a 35% turnover rate here. Roughly 25% is voluntary and the other 10% are people who have been fired for violating our attendance policy. So even if you say something about everyone coming back late everyone knows there's nothing you will do about it."

"But what if I don't make my productivity numbers because people are abusing their breaks and lunches?" asked Frankie.

"Oh Frankie don't become one of them."

"What do you mean? What are you talking about?" Asked Frankie.

"Making your numbers is not the goal. Making your numbers is the process by which we achieve the goal," informed Sheila. "I suggest you mention something to your crew first thing tomorrow. But I also need to tell you that in the future the best way to address these things is immediately when you recognize them. Consequences must be certain and they must be immediate otherwise they lose their impact on changing behaviors. Now I have to run to another meeting but thanks for stopping by."

Frankie pondered what she said. She still didn't quite understand it. She would talk it over with Joe and get his insight. The one takeaway she understood was addressing the issue sooner rather than later. She decided she would talk to the crew before the end of the shift.

"Wow this place is screwed up," she thought to herself.

"Duke we have a small problem. We came up with corrective action plan that will eliminate the possibility of this accident happening again but it points to a management policy change and not an employee mistake." Mike explained, "If we submit the paperwork like that it will affect our discretionary management bonus pool which factors in safety incidents caused by management in a negative way."

"Just fill out the paperwork like all the other ones. Employee coached, Safety bulletin distributed, etc. What's the problem, Mike?"

"Well the problem is I doubt Frankie would sign off on that. The OSHA paperwork requires the incident investigation team to sign off on the corrective action."

"All you need are three signatures. Who participated?"

"Well there was me, Patrick, John, Sheila and Frankie."

"There you go. You, Patrick and John sign off on it. John is just as guilty as anyone here. I heard John told the guy to go break the conveyor jam in the first place. He'd have no problem signing something that points to employee behavior being the accident cause." Duke said.

"OK but what about Sheila? She keeps all the safety incident reports and OSHA paperwork."

"Looks like I'm promoting you. You are now responsible for maintaining safety for our site. When the paperwork comes back from legal sit on it a few days and then I'll announce the organizational change. Sheila will turnover all the files to you and then she will never see it.

"Got it boss." Acknowledged Mike.

15

"Thank you everyone. I just wanted to have a quick crew meeting before then end of shift. Congratulations to everyone for there hard work. We released 100% of all expedited freight orders on time. Just a reminder, breaks are only 10 minutes and lunch is only 30 minutes. Lastly great job on making our numbers today. Despite being short handed you managed to hit our productivity numbers. Thanks again. Have a good night and we'll see you tomorrow."

"What was that about?" asked Tim. Even though he was not carrying that disgusting glass mug, the puffed lower lip was evidence enough that he had tobacco in his mouth.

"Excuse me?" Frankie replied.

"You just fed your crew a shit sandwich." Replied Tim. It was hard not to look at the bits of tobacco on and in between his yellowing teeth. "You just gave them two compliments with a pile of shit in the middle. No matter how sweet the bread it's still a shit sandwich. What do you think they are going to remember about your words?"

"Well as a manager I had to say something. Everyone came back from lunch late today."

"Remember my advice? Find out strengths and weakness, don't play favorites and don't piss off your people. You just broke rule number 3. Why do you think that they come back a little late? You know how far it is from the lunchroom to this area, 7 maybe 10 minutes. Management cut costs by not installing bathrooms or a break area in the new addition. I'm sure it helped them make budget but the consequences are costing them much, much more. You're just lucky you did not say anything at the beginning of the shift or your productivity would have been shot."

"I didn't think about it from that perspective." Replied Frankie.

"Tim get back to work!" growled Wolf from a distance. Tim wandered back to his workstation as Wolf rapidly approached Frankie.

Wolf began a loud belly laugh, "What happened today?"

"What do you mean?" Frankie asked.

"Well everyone's calling it the 'bullshit meeting'. Apparently the name comes from you yelling out bullshit at the top of your lungs." Wolf explained.

"Oh that sounds like a bit of an exaggeration. I may have said something like that. I just felt that Mike was leading us down the wrong path and I interjected my viewpoint. That's all." Said Frankie, "It was nothing really."

"Hey Wolf," asks Frankie, "Is there any reason I couldn't get a picnic table from the lunch room and put them here by my desk where there is some free space?"

"Hell this is second shift. You could do whatever you want." Wolf laughed again.

"Could you help? Do you think you could put in a maintenance request to bring a picnic table over here?"

"Frankie, I like you. Let me give you some advice. Maintenance requests are a 1st shift document. On 2nd shift we just do it. Consider it done. Now go home and get some sleep."

16

The wind felt sharp and brisk. The cold autumn air chilled Frankie but Wolf's actions warmed her. She could not believe her eyes. She could not believe what Wolf had done while she slept. Surrounding her desk were two picnic benches and a vending machine. "Wolf out did himself," she smiled.

The staff meeting was moved to Tuesday because Duke was feeling sick. Everyone is speculating he had a case of the Blue-sky Flu because the temperature hit a high of 75F yesterday. A noticeable raccoon face on Duke confirmed this – red cheeks with a white-eye mask.

"Patrick what have the auditors from MDG found?"

"Well we have not missed an expedited package since they got here." Said Patrick proudly.

"Great work," complimented Duke. There were smiles all around the table as everyone basked in the rare praise from Duke.

Mike however was not so proud. He knew they didn't do anything to fix the problem. The success was an anomaly that would come back to bite them eventually. Hopefully that was well after the auditors left.

Frankie felt good. She knew her direction to Cameron was the main reason expedited freight was on time but she just kept it to herself.

"They are however finding a bunch of packing errors which seem to be a result of incorrect picking." The cheery mood quickly changed.

"God damn it! What are we doing about it?" Growled Duke.

Mike interjected, "Well we are catching everything at the QC table at the end of the line. We think those errors are not exactly picking errors we think the problem was really a result of the conveyor belt jamming and totes dumping orders all over the belt. Today is the first day of not drying the line and we are allowing a flexible start time so there is not a huge influx of boxes and totes before the packaging line starts up. So thanks to Frankie we may have killed two birds with one stone."

"I want to know at the end of each shift any errors that those damn auditors find. I understand MDG is making a visit again next week and I want to have a perfect report card."

17

Duke was all smiles. It had been over a week of zero missed expedited freight and no incorrect shipments going out the door. The few picking errors were caught in final inspection and found to be the result of a part marking issue in the factory. In other words – not Duke's problem.

"Good morning, Reuben. Thanks for coming." Duke met him at the door with visitor badge in hand. "Do you want to meet with your auditors, walk the floor with me or talk in my office."

"I need to talk to my guys first. Then we can walk the floor together. I can't stay long because I have another meeting nearby in a couple hours." Replied Reuben.

It was killing Duke. He really wanted to ask whom his meeting was with. But deep down he knew it could only be with his competitor.

"No worries. Go speak with your guys and when you're ready I will be waiting in my office."

"The picking errors have almost completely vanished. The few we have been finding were really manufacturing problems: mislabeled boxes, wrong items inside boxes. Nothing that really can be blamed on them." Informed Trevor the lead auditor.

"And nothing that will help us break our lease even if we reach a good deal with Maltese." Thought Reuben. "What have they done to improve things?" asked Reuben.

"Well all we can say for sure is that they promoted a new manager, Frankie. She replaced Gary. On the process side they eliminated the policy to dry the line. This seems to have helped tremendously with the picking errors. In fact the picking errors were really a result of boxes getting mixed up when the conveyor jams. I'm not sure what they did to address expedited freight but we haven't found any problems since we arrived."

"Mr. Regus, Reuben is here to see you."
"Of course, send him in."

"Reuben, please have a seat. How did your meeting go? Anything to report?" Duke was smiling inside. He knew they had been meeting expectations and Mike tipped him off about the few errors really being manufacturing issues. Add that to the fact that expedited freight was in 100% compliance. Duke was bracing himself for a compliment from the customer but it never came.

"Duke let's walk the line. I have an issue that has come up from some of our strategic clients. It seems that special instructions are being missed on the packing orders."

They walked out of his office and Duke instructed Linda to have Mike and Patrick meet him on the packing line. As they walked to the other end of the warehouse Duke received a text message from Linda saying that Mike and Patrick were on a conference call with another client but would probably be done in a few minutes.

"Dammit" Duke thought. I don't want to be out here unarmed. He saw Frankie walking in the same direction just in front of him.

"Frankie," he yelled. "Come her a minute. I want to introduce you to our client. Reuben this is Frankie one of our newest managers. Frankie this is Reuben."

After pleasantries were exchanged Duke asked Frankie to join them on their tour of the packing line.

"The issue we are hearing from our clients is that special instructions are being missed. Some customer's request individual labels or slightly different packaging than the standard. They pay extra for these special instructions so it is important that we meet them. In the cases which we get complaints sales is quick to credit them the cost of their shipping which eats into margins."

They scanned the orders queuing on the conveyor belt looking for something with special instructions. They walked the length of the belt all the way to the end where packages and boxes were stacked on pallets for their journey to the different carriers.

Reuben grabbed a package just to show them where on the order label he was talking about.

"Here is where special instructions are written. It's important that your folks look for any message there before sending out to the customer."

"Frankie make a note and make sure that you follow-up with your peers in packing to make sure we have a corrective action procedure in place."

As Duke was issuing orders Reuben noticed a tote full of expedited freight under the conveyor belt. He bent down to take a closer look. The expression on his face said everything Duke needed to know.

"Duke why are there packages here? They were to be delivered today and they are not even on the outbound expedited freight pallet."

Duke didn't have an answer. He turned to look at Frankie. She didn't know what to say.

"I have to head to another meeting. But these are the kinds of problems which are bothering me and bothering my customers and it is the reason we are considering breaking our lease and moving our products down the street." Reuben walked away leaving Duke and Frankie staring at each other.

"Frankie I want this expedited freight issue sorted. That is your number one priority. Do you understand?"

"Yes, Duke I will follow-up right away."

"And that business about moving product down the street. That was just an idle threat. Don't mention it to anyone. That type of rumor could cause a lot of grief."

18

As she inventoried the packages she couldn't help but notice that it was worse than last time. Much worse. There had to be close to 50 packages. All would be late.

"Frankie, what are you doing here? Are you back on second shift?" asked Wolf.

"No I'm just trying to sort out a problem we're having with expedited freight." Responded Frankie.

"Sounds like Duke crapped all over you again. You have a habit of being in the wrong place at the wrong time."

"Yeah I do. Hey, by the way, I guess I'm doing my job. I forgot to tell you that I found my name written on the back of the bathroom stall door. It was a bit hurtful – the picture of me and the words…"

"Oh don't take it personal. It is usually just envy or ignorance. Nothing you can control. Look to tell you the truth. Sometimes I just write bad things about myself on the bathroom walls. It gives me a little bit more authority and clout around here. Could you do me a favor and write a few negative things about me in the ladies room? I'm running out of wall space in the men's room."

What a character he was. "I'll see what I can do. Right now I need to investigate these expedited freight problems."

She waited around for Cameron. After a few minutes she asked someone working in the same area. "Excuse me. Do you know where Cameron is?"

"Whose Cameron? I'm just a temp and I started last night."

She found the manager for the area, "Frankie, Cameron left for the competitor. They are paying 50 cents more per hour plus a second shift bonus. Friday was his last day. Now that word's out I wouldn't be surprised if I lose half my second shift."

Frankie realized she had put in a Band-Aid fix. By asking one person to be responsible was no way to ensure the integrity of a system. She sat down at her desk and tried asking the 5 why's to get to the root cause of this problem.

After staring at a mostly blank page she kept coming to the conclusion that it should just be someone's responsibility but she learned that only works as long as that person stays with the company and never takes vacation or sick leave. That's not a long-term solution. When a problem is solved the solution as well as the problem needs to be shared with everyone.

She reviewed her brown paper that mapped out the packing process. She noticed that expedited freight orders were cut off at 1PM. That would give plenty of time for the orders to be picked and packed before the end of first shift. "Why should second shift be involved at all?" she thought.

After she was satisfied with her root cause analysis and corrective action she sent a note to Duke with a copy to Mike and Patrick. She would explain the plan once she got in tomorrow morning. She couldn't believe the time. It was close to 7PM. Hopefully her family would understand.

19

Frankie pulled in the driveway and noticed not a light was on. That's when it dawned on her that tonight was her son's second basketball game.

"Oh no. I don't want to miss his game again." She quickly made her way back to the car and began heading toward school. She scuffled into the gymnasium only to hear the clock expire.

She found Joe in the stands. "You missed a nail biter, baby. It was a great game and they won this time."

"How'd he do?" she asked.

"Well. He scored a few points but he fouled out late in the third quarter. He seems to play basketball defense like he's playing football. By my count he should have fouled out by the end of the first quarter."

"Oh I can't believe I missed it. I'm sorry. I got caught up with a problem at work."

"Don't worry there'll be more games. Why don't we take the kids out of pizza?"

Over pizza and coke Frankie laughed about the highlights of the game, which Joe described to the best of his memory while the kids inhaled their dinners.

Their youngest let out a loud belch that could be heard throughout the dining area. Frankie was quick to scold while Joe giggled. "Brian Patrick Cabrini! How dare you!"

"Excuse me. Sorry mama."

"Sorry doesn't cut it. I don't ever want to hear that again. And as for you Joe don't encourage him."

As she drove home alone in silence (the boys always preferred driving with their father) she thought about the incident in the restaurant and how it correlated to what was happening at work. She and Joe sending conflicting messages was the same as the managers who dealt with the issue of long lunches in different ways. And her yelling at her son was good in that it was immediate but in reality that's all she ever did. There was really no consequence for his inappropriate behavior. She needed to make sure that she explained to her kids that there would be consequences, like no video games, and when that happened again that she was immediate and certain to act on it.

20

"Frankie nice report. Thorough and to the point. Mike and Patrick implement this immediately. Sheila make sure the job descriptions are revised." Ordered Duke. "We cannot afford to have any shipping errors on the MDG account. Meeting adjourned. Mike, Patrick, Don and John I need you to stick around for a couple minutes more."

The rest of the management team filed out but their heads were still in the conference room. What were they going to discuss? Something was going on and it wasn't good news.

"Wolf what do you think is going on? What do you think they're talking about in there?"

"Hell Frankie, it doesn't take a rocket scientist to see what's going on. We're in deep shit with MDG. I'll bet they're going to Maltese down the street and Duke doesn't have the balls to tell us. And if that happens were all in deep shit. We won't need 25% of the people and we certainly won't need 25% of the managers." Wolf said.

"How did you know that?"

"Frankie, look around. MDG management has been here three weeks in a row. They have had auditors here for the last two weeks in a row. They didn't even spend this much time here when we first got this account."

"Well Duke told me not to say anything but when Reuben was here last he told me these shipping errors are the reason they are considering moving down the street."

"Frankie, that's old news. Do you think that no one else witnessed that exchange between Duke and Reuben? That's what started the rumor in the first place. What confirms it for me is that MDG keeps coming back but only stays here for a few hours tops. Do you think they would fly all the way up from Florida for a couple hours to break our balls? No, they're negotiating with Maltese."

"Shouldn't Duke say something to us if that's the case?"

"Of course he should. But just because he should doesn't mean he will." Responded Wolf.

Campbell, Camerer & Guyette

21

Don explained, "Even if we get rid of 30% of the workforce the numbers show our fixed overheads are going to eliminate are margins. MDG leaving will be detrimental to this business unit unless we get another company in to replace them."

"Well there really is nothing in our sales pipeline. We grew faster than we thought when we moved here. And with the MDG account requiring that addition we thought we would be close to capacity through 2020." Added Mike.

The mood was somber. John needed his job. His wife was expecting but she didn't want to tell her parents just yet. Duke would, no doubt, be thrilled. He always said grandchildren had all the benefits of children without the work or responsibility.

"Gentlemen we need to reconvene this meeting. I have to play golf."

"Dusty. It's Duke. How about we play hooky and get in 9 holes before it starts snowing."

"Hey Duke. Great idea. I think I can sneak away. I'll meet you there. Front nine or back?"

"Front. I have a score to settle with that par 5 on the fourth hole. That bitch has cost me a sleeve a balls every week."

"I know it well. Dropped a few in the drink myself. See you at the first hole."

Duke had been selling third party logistics to Dusty all summer. Not in a pushy way. Just slowly dripping on him every chance he got. Less cost, more flexibility. He knew he had gotten through to him but didn't want to push until he had available capacity to take on another big client. Looks like he was going to be getting that additional capacity without the building addition he had considered for next summer.

The wide open blue sky gave the impression of a warm day but that was the cover for a crisp fall afternoon. Except for the wind it made for great golfing because the course was empty.

"Duke, sorry I'm running a late. Logistics problems."

Those words were music to Duke's ears. He smiled on the inside. On the outside he said, "No worries. You're up. Let's go before the sun stops cooperating."

Dusty's cell phone rang before he could get his driver out of his golf bag. "Excuse me Duke I have to grab this. Some how we misplaced a trailer full of tires."

Duke was on fire. He was feeling good and playing great. He knew it was time to make the ask. As Duke drove the cart toward hole number 4 Dusty wrote down their scores.

"Duke another birdy. Nice."

"So tell me Dusty, how do you misplace a whole trailer full of tires?"

"Geez. Tell me about it. Sometimes I think our own internal suppliers treat us worse than anybody. They forget the goal. We are a customer. We just happen to wear the same badge."

Duke thought, "Now's my chance. I need to make the ask."

"Dusty, let me take over your logistics for commodities like tires. We could stage them for you, manage the inventory and you could work on your golf game knowing we won't lose them."

"I'd like that. But you told me this summer you were

over capacity and that you weren't planning to add capacity until next year. My problems are now. I need a quick fix. After you told me about the benefits of 3PL you got me excited about it as a solution but when you told me you didn't have excess capacity I called Maltese."

"What? Don't tell me you're using those guys?"

"No we're not. But I did meet with them. And you know what? They are over capacity. They told me they didn't have a single free pallet space available and it would be over a year before they could serve a portion of our needs."

"Over capacity? So they don't have a single available pallet space? There's no way MDG can move to Maltese. Either MDG didn't know or they were bluffing me. Either way they're not leaving. At least not this year." Thought Duke.

22

The sun hung low in the sky. The warm fall day quickly became a crisp cool evening. Frankie wrapped herself in her arms as she swiftly walked to her car. She was feeling happy to have contributed to the changes that had led to improved safety, better quality and on-time delivery but she was concerned that it was all for nothing. If MDG left she wouldn't have her management job and she probably wouldn't have her old job either. The drive home passed in the blink of an eye.

"Did you figure out what the goal was yet?"

"How am I supposed to know? You're the college boy. I'm just a working girl." Responded Frankie.

"Damn. I haven't figured it out yet. No one in my

class has either. I found a book called The Goal. But it said the same thing most of my classmates said about the goal being to make profits."

"When I mentioned that to my professor he said stop reading that rubbish until you understand what the real goal is!"

"And I thought to myself what the hell does that mean. Then he went on rambling 'Fish discover water last. The evidence is overwhelming. The evidence is all around you.' Then I just swam away like the little fish that I am."

"Maybe asking the Five Why's can help us figure it out? Why do we have businesses?"

"Well let's think about it in the context of my job."

"OK fine. Why do we have locksmiths?"

"Well most of my work seems to be opening doors that are locked."

"Why do we open doors that are locked?"

"To let in the owners."

"Why do we let in owners?"

"Because they are the ones paying me."

"Why are they paying you?"

"Because they are the customer and they pay us after we serve them."

"Oh my God. That's it."

"What's it? We still have one more why to ask."

"No it's called five why. Doesn't mean you'll always

get to five before you reach of a solution. And I think we have the solution."

"We do?"

"Yes. The purpose of a locksmith is to serve the customer. When you do that you make money. So the purpose of business is to serve the customer!" Frankie was excited. Joe was confused. "How could that be right? It's too simple."

"Ask your teacher. He told you the evidence was all around you. That's why you couldn't see it. Send him an email!"

23

The thunder storm watch concerned Mike but the MDG situation consumed him. He couldn't eat, sleep or concentrate. All he could think about was the ramifications of losing them as a customer. Duke's attitude and behavior just made matters worse. He didn't seem to care in the least. He had to confront him on this issue.

"Duke can I talk to you for a minute?" Asked Mike softly as his hair fell in front of his eyes.

"Come on in. What's up? Besides the fact that you need a comb or haircut or both." Duke ribbed him. He was in the best mood he'd been in in quite awhile.

"Frankly, Duke, everyone's concerned about MDG. And our future without them. Then yesterday you leave to go play golf. People are saying you're off your rocker. And with the seriousness of the situation I think we need to let corporate know what's going on and the PE investors before the next quarterly board meeting."

"Oh Mike. Relax. You worry too much. I've got it all under control. I sent a note to corporate giving them a complete update on the situation. They called after receiving it and had a few follow-up questions but my answers put them at ease. I doubt it will even be a topic at the next board meeting."

"But Duke how can you be so sure?" pleaded Mike. "If they announce a move we'll be fired so fast…

"Jesus, Mike, relax. Sometimes you suffer from diarrhea of the mouth and constipation of the brain!"

"But Duke look at the evidence: We know they're meeting with Maltese. One of our best guys takes a job there, probably telling them how to set everything up so they can flip the switch whenever they want."

"Dammit Mike! I have got this under control!", Duke calmed himself and softly continued, "In fact, so much so guess who they want to lead the expansion in Savannah?"

"What?"

"That's right I'm going to Savannah beginning next month. And guess what? You're coming with me."

24

Joe sat in annoyed silence staring at the screen of his desktop pc while it booted up. He sat pondering the question of whether all the efficiencies from PC's are voided by the wasted time waiting for them to turn on and off. After what felt like an eternity he clicked on the message from his professor.

"Yes Joe! You are correct. The try-angle approach we've been discussing – the system, the problem solving, the knowledge sharing, the leadership – all those capabilities are vital but they're meaningless without a customer to serve. The purpose of business is to serve the customer. The *real goal* is to serve the customer. Making money is the result of doing that well!" wrote back Joe's professor.

"Well I'll be damned. You're right Frankie. That was it."

25

Frankie subconsciously knew what the goal was but now it was forefront. In order to make money she needed to make sure she and her peers were serving the customer. When the MDG turnaround agenda item came up at the staff meeting she was prepared to speak up.

"So guys our insurance company has reached a settlement with the widow, so thank God we're not going to court on that. That's the good news. The bad news is – I'm leaving." Duke left a dramatic pause in the air so he wouldn't miss the reaction.

The reaction was not as impressive as Duke imagined it in his head but he knew that they had to be surprised even if they did not outwardly express it. "That's right. You may have heard me discuss the expansion project. The company has decided to build a new facility near the Savannah port. I will be leading that project and Mike will be joining me. So that probably leaves you wondering who will take over our jobs?"

"Well I have not decided yet. But that will be my last decision here. I will announce it before the end of the month. That's it from my side."

"Duke," Frankie interrupted, "We skipped over the MDG turnaround plan agenda item."

"That situation is under control. Really nothing to report there. That agenda was put together before some recent developments and I just never sent out a revised agenda."

One of the timid managers who hardly ever said anything spoke up, "I heard they were going to our competitor."

"Well that is complete nonsense. And that's why I don't like rumors. The fact is we have made some errors." Frankie imagined Duke's nose was growing as he spoke. "Small errors. But those have been corrected for the most part. More importantly they could not go to our competitor because they are over capacity and if they were to put up more bricks and mortar we're talking over a year before they could even consider taking on a new client. So in the short run there is nothing to worry about."

The answer satisfied everyone except Frankie. "Well even if that's the case, it's the long run that matters. I have some ideas that I think will improve the customer relationship."

"OK Frankie, you have the floor." Duke glanced at his watch thinking there would still be time for a late afternoon round on the back nine. He was done donating balls to the water hazard on 4.

"Thanks Duke. What's the goal of business?" she asked with a flare of drama.

Almost in unison Don and Duke replied, "To make a money."

"No!" Frankie yelled back. She set them up and they fell in her trap. Her loud vocal response startled them all even Duke. "The real goal of business is to serve the customer and make money is the result of doing that well. Customers demand total satisfaction and they measure it in terms of quality, cost, delivery, safety and morale. We have been lacking in every one of those categories in our efforts to serve MDG. I got to thinking that we have been too reactive. We need to be proactive and rebuild this relationship with MDG."

"What are you proposing Frankie? I already offered them our Cubs tickets. They didn't want that. Get to the point." Interjected Duke. No one was going to hijack his staff meeting or his opportunity to sneak in 9 holes.

"Now that we have improved our quality issues, reduced our overtime and met our expedited freight orders we need to make them feel safe about being our customers. We need to give them piece of mind that we are serving them. We need to make them happy to be our customer. I'm proposing that we work together them. Especially with their auditors. Instead of trying to hide problems from them we should share knowledge with them and ask for their help in solving problems."

Duke couldn't believe his ears but didn't care either because he knew that he was gone in a few weeks and that this would be someone else's problem. He did not want to extend this discussion any longer. He had nine holes in front of him.

"Frankie, great ideas," lied Duke. "Go ahead and implement your ideas. You work personally with those auditors. Meeting adjourned."

26

When the boys fell asleep the house was so quiet that Frankie in bed on the third floor could faintly hear the sound of the washing machine in its spin cycle in the basement. Joe was all eyes and ears focused on the sports channel plays of the day. Frankie was bursting to tell him about her day but she knew where his focus was. She flirted with the idea of taking off her shirt to see if he'd notice.

When the count down got to five she blurted, "Joe you should have heard me in the staff meeting today. I asked them what the real goal of business was and both Don and Duke said to make money. I yelled back that they were wrong and it felt so good. Then I told them what the real goal was and my plan for repairing our customer relationship. Oh, and by the way Duke's leaving and I am a candidate to replace him. And so

I started working with the auditors…

"What?!!" interjected Joe who she thought was watching sports center and not really paying any attention anyway.

"I started to say I am working with the auditors to address…"

"No back up. Before that."

"Oh Duke's leaving and Shelia told me she put my name in as a part of the succession plan."

"Are you kidding me? A VP job? How much does that pay?"

"I don't know, $150K. I think. It's not about the money. I'm honored that I'm being considered. And besides I don't think I have much of a chance because I don't have much management experience."

"Excuse me. At that salary it damn well is about the money. What do you need to do to get the job?"

"It's out of my control. It's Duke's decision. He's considering candidates and will make an announcement at the end of the month."

27

The autumn blue moon hung in the sky opposite the rising sun. The dancing light reflected off the shiny asphalt parking lot. The black ice was a sign that winter was coming. The brisk wind was evidence it would be here soon.

Duke stood hands on his hips. He anxiously awaited his most high maintenance customer. This impromptu customer visit caused him to miss a corporate boondoggle. He didn't understand why his boss insisted that he be there personally but he did know how to read an organization chart.

"Reuben, glad you could come out to visit us again." Said Duke. "I was surprised to hear you were coming so early this morning. Don't you usually take the morning flight?"

"Actually Duke, I do but I came here yesterday to visit a client that is pleased with our turnaround. I came here this morning to meet Frankie. I think I probably didn't leave a good first impression as I walked out last time without saying good-bye. She's doing a fantastic job so say my auditors. They have worked together to make several small improvements which has improved quality and I understand also improved your productivity. And our strategic accounts have never been happier."

"That's right. Our costs are down and our throughput is up." Responded Duke.

"Well those quality and delivery improvements are why we are accelerating our plan to move additional volume here. And I want to personally thank Frankie for her help in giving me the confidence to make that decision."

"Oh Frankie. Yes, I took her under my wing as soon as I promoted her." Boasted Duke.

Reuben could see through the bullshit. "Duke, I understand from my team that you're moving back to corporate."

"That's half true. I'm moving to lead 'Project Boat to Throat'. It's our new fresh food warehouse that will be responsible for picking up fresh produce at the ships in the port, cross docking at our facility and then dispatching to independent grocers in and around Atlanta. I came up with the project name," said Duke proudly.

"Catchy name." replied Reuben. "Look my point is

that Frankie has a lot to do with us continuing to keep our business here and she has everything to do with us expanding it. I think she would be an excellent candidate to fill your shoes."

"Thanks Reuben. She has been one of the best I've mentored. I have not made a decision yet but I will tell you this – she is on the short list of three. It would be out of line and premature for me to say anything more."

28

Rumors had been blowing throughout the warehouse like leaves on a brisk fall day. Even though she had only been a manager a short time many were picking Frankie to take over for Duke. It had already been announced that Mike was joining him on that project which eliminated him from the field of potential replacements.

People were divided into one of three certainties. The first group was certain corporate would be sending in the next GM. The second group thought it would be Patrick and the last group felt it should be Frankie.

Frankie never dreamed of being the VP and GM of the whole facility. Her husband always dreamed of a six-figure income and company car. He just never dreamed it would come true or that his wife would be the one with the title and the company car.

This was the first staff meeting Frankie attended in her short management career where everyone was early. You could feel the tension and the excitement in the room. It was masked slightly by the nervous conversations and the occasional well-wishers to both front runners Patrick and Frankie.

"Well Frankie," said Wolf, "looks like it's down to you and Patrick. If it were a corporate stiff he would have been here or Sheila would've known. So I may be kissing your ass soon."

"Wolfie, that's what I wrote about you in the ladies room." Frankie whispered.

"Ha ha ha," belly laughed Wolf, "Good luck. In all seriousness you deserve it. You have right combination of expertise and empathy. You will go far. But when you're my boss don't you dare take me off second shift."

The room hushed quiet when Duke opened the door. "Gentlemen and ladies. You all know I am not much for words so I'll be brief."

Duke didn't even sit down. He was wearing a golf shirt that barely covered his beer gut and only stayed tucked in when he stood still. He tucked his shirt back in and said, "As this is the last time we'll be meeting together as a team I wanted to publicly thank Frankie for all her help in keeping MDG a happy customer. Frankie, without you who knows where we'd

The Real Goal

be today. On the subject of my successor I want to tell you that it was not an easy decision. After long thought and deliberation I've decided that John will be taking over effective tomorrow. Again thank you all for your help over these last few years and I hope our career paths cross again."

Mike broke the awkward silence by clapping. Although everyone else reluctantly joined him on the outside, they were stunned on the inside. The look of shock stood still in their faces.

"Wolf I think I just bit into a opened-face shit sandwich." Whispered Frankie.

"We all just bit into a shit sandwich. John, his son in law? He couldn't find his way out of a wet paper bag."

"Shush, Wolf, keep it down so your new boss doesn't hear you."

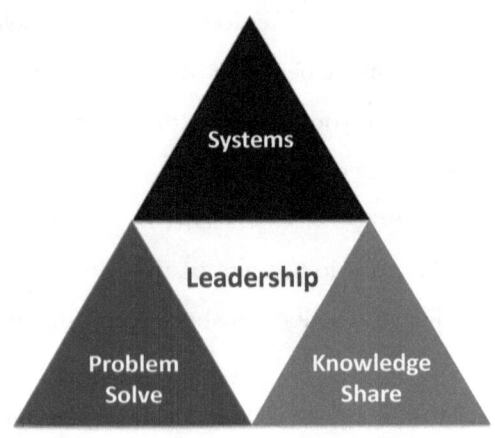

TRY-ANGLE

This equilateral try-angle symbolizes our approach to operational excellence. The four interior triangles represent the essential elements:

Leadership – we think of leadership not in the traditional sense of formal leaders. We think of leadership as something that is everyone's responsibiilty. Everyone has the responsibility to step-up to leadership when the opportunity arises. Formal leaders have the responsibility to create the environment in which everyone has the opportunity to pursue autonomy, mastery and purpose. This upside down triangle is like the greek letter delta or change. It is everyone's responsibility to initiate, create and support change.

Systems – every business is a summation of processes that make up the system by which customers are served. Every system starts out simple and linear. Over time they have a tendency to become tangled webs that create confusion, steel traps that nothing escapes and sieves that leak profits. Leaders at all levels must understand these systems to make the complex simple again and they must optimize them for the good of the customer.

Problem Solving – most problem solving is superficial, never really getting to the root cause. Suppliers bend over backwards to solve a customer complaint but never put the time and energy into making sure that problem doesn't come back again. Root cause analysis is merely a phrase thrown around by managers.

Knowledge sharing – Sharing knowledge amongst workers and clients is the single biggest opportunity to reduce the waste of searching for information. We need to better link those in need of information to those with knowledge.

We think of Operational Excellence as the summation of Strategy plus Alignment. We define alignment as the product of character, competence and collaboration.

Our character is the summation of our behaviors. Our behaviors are a reflection of our values. Together, behavior and values, make up our company culture. As Drucker said, "Culture eats Strategy for breakfast." Strategy alone is not enough to change a culture.

We help businesses by holding up a mirror to their culture. With that starting-point we work together to define or to re-fine their strategies. Then we collaborate with all levels of the organization to align them to that strategy.

Our Vision Is To Be The CXO's Secret Weapon.

Our Mission Is To Lead small Teams To BIG Results.

ABOUT THE

AUTHORS

Terry L. Campbell is an Operations Consultant for OpEx. He is an Iraq War vet who was responsible for supply chain management for mission critical equipment, weaponry and ammunition. He grew up on the south side of Chicago but today he calls south Florida home. He can be reached at TerryCampbell@4OpEx.com

James Camerer, Jr. is an Operations Consultant for OpEx. He is a two-time Iraq War vet. He brings his years of military logistics, fleet management and operations experience to clients in the Manufacturing and Distribution industries. He lives in St. Louis, Mo. He can be reached at JamesCamerer@4OpEx.com

James M. Guyette, Jr. is Managing Director of North American Operations for OpEx. He combines years of practical manufacturing industry experience with years of strategy, operations and engineering consulting experience to various industries around the world. He calls Chicago's Lakeview neighborhood home. He can be reached at JamesGuyette@4OpEx.com